40
AND
PROUD
OF IT

summersdale

40 AND PROUD OF IT

Copyright © Summersdale Publishers Ltd, 2014

With text contributed by Vicky Edwards

All rights reserved.

Summersdale Publishers Ltd
46 West Street
Chichester
West Sussex
PO19 1RP
UK

www.summersdale.com

Printed and bound in the Czech Republic

ISBN: 978-1-84953-562-5

Substantial discounts on bulk quantities of Summersdale books are available to corporations, professional associations and other organisations. For details contact Nicky Douglas by telephone: +44 (0) 1243 756902, fax: +44 (0) 1243 786300 or email: nicky@summersdale.com.

TO...

FROM...

CONTENTS

ANOTHER YEAR OLDER

LIFE BEGINS AT 40.

W. B. Pitkin

I'M 40 AND I FEEL GREAT. FEEL FOR YOURSELF!

Anonymous

THE LOVELY THING ABOUT BEING 40 IS THAT YOU CAN APPRECIATE 25-YEAR-OLD MEN MORE.

Colleen McCullough

AS A GRADUATE OF
THE ZSA ZSA GABOR
SCHOOL OF CREATIVE
MATHEMATICS, I
HONESTLY DO NOT KNOW
HOW OLD I AM.

Erma Bombeck

THERE WAS A STAR DANCED, AND UNDER THAT WAS I BORN.

William Shakespeare

OUR BIRTHDAYS ARE
FEATHERS IN THE BROAD
WING OF TIME.

Jean Paul

LIKE MANY WOMEN MY AGE, I AM 28 YEARS OLD.

Mary Schmich

WHEN I PASSED 40 I
DROPPED PRETENCE,
'CAUSE MEN LIKE
WOMEN WHO GOT
SOME SENSE.

Maya Angelou

THIS WINE IS 40 YEARS
OLD. IT CERTAINLY
DOESN'T SHOW ITS AGE.

Cicero

FORTY IS GREAT –
IT'S THE NINETEENTH
ANNIVERSARY OF YOUR
TWENTY-FIRST!

Anonymous

WE DON'T UNDERSTAND
LIFE ANY BETTER AT 40
THAN AT 20, BUT WE
KNOW IT AND ADMIT IT.

Jules Renard

EVERY YEAR ON YOUR BIRTHDAY, YOU GET A CHANCE TO START NEW.

Sammy Hagar

WOMEN ARE MOST
FASCINATING BETWEEN
THE AGES OF 35 AND
40... SINCE FEW WOMEN
EVER PASS 40, MAXIMUM
FASCINATION CAN
CONTINUE INDEFINITELY.

Christian Dior

IT TAKES A LONG TIME TO BECOME YOUNG.

Pablo Picasso

AT 20 YEARS OF AGE,
THE WILL REIGNS;
AT 30, THE WIT; AND AT
40, THE JUDGEMENT.

Benjamin Franklin

WOMEN DESERVE TO
HAVE MORE THAN 12
YEARS BETWEEN THE
AGES OF 28 AND 40.

James Thurber

AT 15, MY MIND WAS
BENT ON LEARNING. AT
30, I STOOD FIRM. AT
40, I HAD NO DOUBTS.

Confucius

YOU'RE NOT 40; YOU'RE 18 WITH 22 YEARS' EXPERIENCE.

Anonymous

JUST
WHAT
I ALWAYS
WANTED

BIRTHDAYS ARE GOOD
FOR YOU. STATISTICS
SHOW THAT THE PEOPLE
WHO HAVE THE MOST
LIVE THE LONGEST.

Larry Lorenzoni

WHEN IT COMES TO
STAYING YOUNG, A MIND-
LIFT BEATS A FACELIFT
ANY DAY.

Marty Bucella

I DO WISH I COULD
TELL YOU MY AGE BUT
IT'S IMPOSSIBLE.
IT KEEPS CHANGING
ALL THE TIME.

Greer Garson

WHY IS A BIRTHDAY CAKE
THE ONLY FOOD YOU CAN
BLOW ON AND SPIT ON
AND EVERYBODY RUSHES
TO GET A PIECE?

Bobby Kelton

FOR MY FORTIETH I ASKED HER FOR A DIRTY WEEKEND. SHE GAVE ME A TRIP TO THE BRITISH BOG-SNORKELLING CHAMPIONSHIPS.

Anonymous

A WISE LOVER VALUES
NOT SO MUCH THE GIFT
OF THE LOVER AS THE
LOVE OF THE GIVER.

Thomas à Kempis

YOUTH IS THE GIFT OF NATURE, BUT AGE IS A WORK OF ART.

Garson Kanin

YESTERDAY IS HISTORY,
TOMORROW IS A
MYSTERY, BUT TODAY
IS A GIFT. THAT IS WHY
IT IS CALLED
THE PRESENT.

Eleanor Roosevelt

PLEAS'D TO LOOK
FORWARD, PLEAS'D TO
LOOK BEHIND,
AND COUNT EACH
BIRTHDAY WITH A
GRATEFUL MIND.

Alexander Pope

A HUG IS THE PERFECT
GIFT: ONE SIZE FITS ALL
AND NOBODY MINDS IF
YOU EXCHANGE IT.

Anonymous

BIRTHDAYS ARE
NATURE'S WAY OF
TELLING US TO EAT
MORE CAKE.

Anonymous

THE BEST BIRTHDAYS ARE ALL THOSE THAT HAVEN'T ARRIVED YET.

Robert Orben

I HAVE EVERYTHING I
HAD 20 YEARS AGO,
ONLY IT'S ALL A
LITTLE BIT LOWER.

Gypsy Rose Lee

THE ABILITY TO
LAUGH, ESPECIALLY AT
OURSELVES, KEEPS THE
HEART LIGHT AND THE
MIND YOUNG.

Anonymous

A GIFT, WITH A KIND
COUNTENANCE, IS A
DOUBLE PRESENT.

Proverb

GRIN
AND
BEAR
IT

I KNEW I WAS GOING
BALD WHEN IT WAS
TAKING ME LONGER AND
LONGER TO WASH
MY FACE.

Harry Hill

AGE IS AN ISSUE OF
MIND OVER MATTER.
IF YOU DON'T MIND, IT
DOESN'T MATTER.

Mark Twain

THE FIRST 40 YEARS OF
LIFE GIVE US THE TEXT;
THE NEXT 30 SUPPLY
THE COMMENTARY ON IT.

Arthur Schopenhauer

WE TURN NOT OLDER
WITH YEARS, BUT NEWER
EVERY DAY.

Emily Dickinson

YOU CAN'T TURN BACK THE CLOCK, BUT YOU CAN WIND IT UP AGAIN.

Bonnie Prudden

YOUTH IS A CIRCUMSTANCE YOU CAN'T DO ANYTHING ABOUT. THE TRICK IS TO GROW UP WITHOUT GETTING OLD.

Frank Lloyd Wright

'AGE' IS THE
ACCEPTANCE OF A
TERM OF YEARS. BUT
MATURITY IS THE GLORY
OF YEARS.

Martha Graham

I BELIEVE IN LOYALTY; I
THINK WHEN A WOMAN
REACHES A CERTAIN AGE
SHE LIKES SHE SHOULD
STICK TO IT.

Eva Gabor

IT'S SAD TO GROW OLD, BUT NICE TO RIPEN.

Brigitte Bardot

YOUTH IS A WONDERFUL THING. WHAT A CRIME TO WASTE IT ON CHILDREN.

George Bernard Shaw

STOP WORRYING ABOUT
THE POTHOLES IN THE
ROAD AND CELEBRATE
THE JOURNEY!

Anonymous

AGEING IS NOT 'LOST YOUTH' BUT A NEW STAGE OF OPPORTUNITY AND STRENGTH.

Betty Friedan

AGE IS SOMETHING
THAT DOESN'T MATTER,
UNLESS YOU ARE A
CHEESE.

Billie Burke

TIME HAS A WONDERFUL WAY OF WEEDING OUT THE TRIVIAL.

Richard Ben Sapir

PUSHING 40?
SHE'S HANGING ON
FOR DEAR LIFE.

Ivy Compton-Burnett

WHEN IT COMES TO AGE
WE'RE ALL IN THE SAME
BOAT, ONLY SOME OF US
HAVE BEEN ABOARD A
LITTLE LONGER.

Leo Probst

THE LONGER I LIVE
THE MORE BEAUTIFUL
LIFE BECOMES.

Frank Lloyd Wright

DO A
LITTLE
DANCE,
MAKE A
LITTLE
LOVE

THE OLDER ONE GROWS, THE MORE ONE LIKES INDECENCY.

Virginia Woolf

I'LL KEEP SWIVELLING
MY HIPS UNTIL THEY
NEED REPLACING.

Tom Jones

THERE'S A KIND OF
CONFIDENCE THAT COMES
WHEN YOU'RE IN YOUR
FORTIES AND FIFTIES,
AND MEN FIND THAT
INCREDIBLY ATTRACTIVE.

Peggy Northrop

NO MATTER WHAT
HAPPENS, I'M LOUD,
NOISY, EARTHY AND
READY FOR MUCH
MORE LIVING.

Elizabeth Taylor

A MAN IS ONLY AS
OLD AS THE WOMAN
HE FEELS.

Groucho Marx

WHEN OUR VICES
DESERT US, WE FLATTER
OURSELVES THAT WE ARE
DESERTING OUR VICES.

François de La Rochefoucauld

I AM NOT OLD
BUT MELLOW
LIKE GOOD WINE.

Stephen Phillips

THE ONLY FORM OF EXERCISE I TAKE IS MASSAGE.

Truman Capote

I'M LIMITLESS AS FAR
AS AGE IS CONCERNED...
AS LONG AS HE HAS A
DRIVER'S LICENCE.

Kim Cattrall
on dating younger men

IT'S SEX, NOT YOUTH, THAT'S WASTED ON THE YOUNG.

Janet Harris

GROW OLD
ALONG WITH ME!
THE BEST IS
YET TO BE.

Robert Browning

LET US CELEBRATE THE
OCCASION WITH WINE
AND SWEET WORDS.

Plautus

I AM GETTING TO AN AGE
WHEN I CAN ONLY ENJOY
THE LAST SPORT LEFT. IT
IS CALLED HUNTING FOR
YOUR SPECTACLES.

Edward Grey

YOUNG
AT
HEART

WHEN CHOOSING
BETWEEN TWO EVILS,
I ALWAYS LIKE TO TRY
THE ONE I'VE NEVER
TRIED BEFORE.

Mae West

IF YOU OBEY ALL THE RULES, YOU MISS ALL THE FUN.

Katharine Hepburn

I'LL GROW OLD
PHYSICALLY, BUT I WON'T
GROW OLD MUSICALLY.

Cliff Richard

MEN CHASE GOLF BALLS
WHEN THEY'RE TOO OLD
TO CHASE ANYTHING
ELSE.

Groucho Marx

THE MORE YOU PRAISE
AND CELEBRATE YOUR
LIFE, THE MORE
THERE IS IN LIFE TO
CELEBRATE.

Oprah Winfrey

I HAVE THE BODY OF AN 18-YEAR-OLD. I KEEP IT IN THE FRIDGE.

Spike Milligan

THE OLDER I GET, THE OLDER OLD IS.

Tom Baker

THE BEST YEARS OF A WOMAN'S LIFE – THE TEN YEARS BETWEEN 39 AND 40.

Anonymous

YOU KNOW YOU ARE
GETTING OLDER WHEN
'HAPPY HOUR' IS A NAP.

Gray Kristofferson

OLD PEOPLE AREN'T EXEMPT FROM HAVING FUN AND DANCING... AND PLAYING.

Liz Smith

IF YOU GIVE UP
SMOKING, DRINKING
AND LOVING, YOU DON'T
ACTUALLY LIVE LONGER,
IT JUST SEEMS LONGER.

Clement Freud

IT'S IMPORTANT TO HAVE
A TWINKLE IN YOUR
WRINKLE.

Anonymous

THE OLDER A MAN GETS,
THE FARTHER HE HAD
TO WALK TO SCHOOL
AS A BOY.

Henry Brightman

SOME KIDS IN ITALY
CALL ME 'MAMA JAZZ';
I THOUGHT THAT WAS
SO CUTE. AS LONG AS
THEY DON'T CALL ME
'GRANDMA JAZZ'.

Ella Fitzgerald

SOMETIMES WHEN A
MAN RECALLS THE GOOD
OLD DAYS, HE'S REALLY
THINKING OF HIS BAD
YOUNG DAYS.

Anonymous

I DON'T PLAN TO GROW
OLD GRACEFULLY; I PLAN
TO HAVE FACELIFTS
UNTIL MY EARS MEET.

Rita Rudner

YOU'LL FIND AS YOU
GROW OLDER THAT YOU
WEREN'T BORN SUCH
A GREAT WHILE AGO
AFTER ALL. THE TIME
SHORTENS UP.

Frank Lloyd Wright

OLDER
AND
WISER?

YOU'RE ONLY AS YOUNG
AS THE LAST TIME YOU
CHANGED YOUR MIND.

Timothy Leary

BE WISE WITH SPEED;
A FOOL AT 40 IS
A FOOL INDEED.

Edward Young

THE BEST THINGS IN
LIFE AREN'T THINGS.

Art Buchwald

KEEP TRUE TO THE DREAMS OF THY YOUTH.

Friedrich von Schiller

NONE ARE SO OLD
AS THOSE WHO HAVE
OUTLIVED ENTHUSIASM.

Henry David Thoreau

OLD AGE IS LIKE A
PLANE FLYING THROUGH
A STORM. ONCE YOU
ARE ABOARD THERE IS
NOTHING YOU CAN DO.

Golda Meir

WISDOM DOESN'T
NECESSARILY COME
WITH AGE. SOMETIMES
AGE JUST SHOWS UP
ALL BY ITSELF.

Tom Wilson

A PRUNE IS AN EXPERIENCED PLUM.

John Trattner

THERE IS NO OLD AGE.
THERE IS, AS THERE
ALWAYS WAS, JUST YOU.

Carol Matthau

IF I HAD TO LIVE MY
LIFE OVER AGAIN,
I'D BE A PLUMBER.

Albert Einstein

A MAN IS NOT OLD AS LONG AS HE IS SEEKING SOMETHING.

Jean Rostand

CHERISH ALL YOUR
HAPPY MOMENTS: THEY
MAKE A FINE CUSHION
FOR OLD AGE.

Christopher Morley

AS WE GROW OLDER, OUR
BODIES GET SHORTER
AND OUR ANECDOTES
LONGER.

Robert Quillen

IF YOU WANT A THING
DONE WELL, GET A
COUPLE OF OLD BROADS
TO DO IT.

Bette Davis

AT AGE 20, WE WORRY
ABOUT WHAT OTHERS
THINK OF US. AT 40, WE
DON'T CARE WHAT THEY
THINK OF US.

Ann Landers

LIVE, LOVE AND LAST

EVERYONE IS THE AGE OF THEIR HEART.

Guatemalan proverb

ONE SHOULD NEVER
MAKE ONE'S DEBUT IN
A SCANDAL. ONE SHOULD
RESERVE THAT TO GIVE
INTEREST TO ONE'S
OLD AGE.

Oscar Wilde

REGULAR NAPS PREVENT OLD AGE, ESPECIALLY IF YOU TAKE THEM WHILE DRIVING.

Anonymous

AGE IS WHATEVER YOU
THINK IT IS. YOU ARE
AS OLD AS YOU THINK
YOU ARE.

Muhammad Ali

NO MATTER HOW OLD YOU ARE, THERE'S ALWAYS SOMETHING GOOD TO LOOK FORWARD TO.

Lynn Johnston

TO STOP AGEING, KEEP ON RAGING.

Michael Forbes

AGE DOES NOT PROTECT
YOU FROM LOVE.
BUT LOVE, TO SOME
EXTENT, PROTECTS
YOU FROM AGE.

Jeanne Moreau

DON'T LET AGEING GET
YOU DOWN. IT'S TOO
HARD TO GET BACK UP.

John Wagner

TOMORROW'S GONE – WE'LL HAVE TONIGHT!

Dorothy Parker

THERE ARE THREE
STAGES OF A MAN'S
LIFE: HE BELIEVES
IN SANTA CLAUS, HE
DOESN'T BELIEVE IN
SANTA CLAUS, HE IS
SANTA CLAUS.

Anonymous

IT'S A GOOD IDEA TO
OBEY ALL THE RULES
WHEN YOU'RE YOUNG
JUST SO YOU'LL HAVE
THE STRENGTH TO
BREAK THEM WHEN
YOU'RE OLD.

Mark Twain

AT MIDDLE AGE THE
SOUL SHOULD BE
OPENING UP LIKE A
ROSE, NOT CLOSING UP
LIKE A CABBAGE.

John Andrew Holmes

HE WHO LAUGHS, LASTS!

Mary Pettibone Poole

ILLS,
PILLS
AND
TWINGES

I KEEP FIT. EVERY
MORNING I DO A
HUNDRED LAPS OF
AN OLYMPIC-SIZED
SWIMMING POOL IN A
SMALL MOTOR LAUNCH.

Peter Cook

AS YOU GET OLDER
THREE THINGS HAPPEN.
THE FIRST IS YOUR
MEMORY GOES, AND I
CAN'T REMEMBER THE
OTHER TWO...

Norman Wisdom

MY MOTHER IS NO
SPRING CHICKEN,
ALTHOUGH SHE HAS GOT
AS MANY CHEMICALS IN
HER AS ONE.

Dame Edna Everage

I DON'T WANT A FLU JAB.
I LIKE GETTING FLU. IT
GIVES ME SOMETHING
ELSE TO COMPLAIN
ABOUT.

David Letterman

MIDDLE AGE IS WHEN
YOU CHOOSE YOUR
CEREAL FOR THE FIBRE,
NOT THE TOY.

Anonymous

I HAVE A FURNITURE
PROBLEM. MY CHEST
HAS FALLEN INTO MY
DRAWERS.

Billy Casper

I'D LIKE TO LEARN TO SKI BUT I'M WORRIED ABOUT MY KNEES. THEY CREAK... AND I'M AFRAID THEY MIGHT START AN AVALANCHE.

Jonathan Ross

WHAT MOST PERSONS
CONSIDER AS VIRTUE,
AFTER THE AGE OF 40
IS SIMPLY A LOSS OF
ENERGY.

Voltaire

I GO SLOWER AS TIME GOES FASTER.

Mason Cooley

NOTHING IS MORE
RESPONSIBLE FOR THE
GOOD OLD DAYS THAN A
BAD MEMORY.

Franklin Pierce Adams

I HOPE TO HAVE IT
REPLACED VERY SOON.

Terry Wogan on people saying that he
didn't know the meaning of 'hip'

THE OLDER THE FIDDLE, THE SWEETER THE TUNE.

English proverb

I DON'T KNOW HOW YOU
FEEL ABOUT OLD AGE...
BUT IN MY CASE I DIDN'T
EVEN SEE IT COMING. IT
HIT ME FROM THE REAR.

Phyllis Diller

THE OLDER YOU GET,
THE MORE YOU TELL IT
LIKE IT USED TO BE.

Anonymous

OLD MINDS ARE LIKE
OLD HORSES; YOU MUST
EXERCISE THEM IF YOU
WISH TO KEEP THEM IN
WORKING ORDER.

John Quincy Adams

CHIN UP, CHEST OUT

A WOMAN PAST 40
SHOULD MAKE UP HER
MIND TO BE YOUNG, AND
NOT HER FACE.

Billie Burke

PROFESSIONALLY, I HAVE NO AGE.

Kathleen Turner

GREY HAIR IS GOD'S GRAFFITI.

Bill Cosby

AS THE ARTERIES
GROW HARD, THE HEART
GROWS SOFT.

H. L. Mencken

INFLATION IS WHEN
YOU PAY 15 DOLLARS FOR
THE 10-DOLLAR HAIRCUT
YOU USED TO GET FOR
5 DOLLARS WHEN YOU
HAD HAIR.

Sam Ewing

WRINKLES ARE
HEREDITARY. PARENTS
GET THEM FROM THEIR
CHILDREN.

Doris Day

AS WE GROW OLD... THE BEAUTY STEALS INWARD.

Ralph Waldo Emerson

THE SPIRITUAL EYESIGHT IMPROVES AS THE PHYSICAL EYESIGHT DECLINES.

Plato

I'M NOT DENYING MY
AGE, I'M EMBELLISHING
MY YOUTH.

Tamara Reynolds

I GUESS I DON'T SO
MUCH MIND BEING OLD,
AS I MIND BEING FAT
AND OLD.

Peter Gabriel

AGE SELDOM ARRIVES
SMOOTHLY OR QUICKLY.
IT'S MORE OFTEN A
SUCCESSION OF JERKS.

Jean Rhys

THE SECRET OF STAYING YOUNG IS TO LIVE HONESTLY, EAT SLOWLY AND LIE ABOUT YOUR AGE.

Lucille Ball

IF YOU WANT TO LOOK
YOUNG AND THIN, HANG
AROUND OLD FAT PEOPLE.

Jim Eason

WRINKLES SHOULD MERELY INDICATE WHERE SMILES HAVE BEEN.

Mark Twain

YOU KNOW YOU'RE
GETTING OLD WHEN YOU
CAN PINCH AN INCH ON
YOUR FOREHEAD.

John Mendoza

MIDDLE AGE IS WHEN
A NARROW WAIST AND A
BROAD MIND BEGIN TO
CHANGE PLACES.

Anonymous

AS YOU GET OLDER, THE
PICKINGS GET SLIMMER,
BUT THE PEOPLE DON'T.

Carrie Fisher

PEOPLE SAY THAT AGE
IS JUST A STATE OF
MIND. I SAY IT'S MORE
ABOUT THE STATE OF
YOUR BODY.

Geoffrey Parfitt

WOMEN ARE NOT
FORGIVEN FOR AGEING.
ROBERT REDFORD'S
LINES OF DISTINCTION
ARE MY OLD-AGE
WRINKLES.

Jane Fonda

THE EASIEST WAY
TO DIMINISH THE
APPEARANCE OF
WRINKLES IS TO KEEP
YOUR GLASSES OFF
WHEN YOU LOOK IN
THE MIRROR.

Joan Rivers

THE MORE SAND HAS
ESCAPED FROM THE
HOURGLASS OF OUR
LIFE, THE CLEARER
WE SHOULD SEE
THROUGH IT.

Jean Paul

YOU ARE NEVER TOO OLD TO SET ANOTHER GOAL OR TO DREAM A NEW DREAM.

C. S. Lewis

@EsmeTheBird

If you're interested in finding out more about our books, find us on Facebook at **Summersdale Publishers** and follow us on Twitter at **@Summersdale**.

www.summersdale.com